American Lives

William Clark

Elizabeth Raum

Heinemann Library
Chicago, Illinois

© 2004 Heinemann Library
a division of Reed Elsevier Inc.
Chicago, Illinois

Customer Service 888-454-2279
Visit our website at www.heinemannlibrary.com

Designed by Sarah Figlio
Photo research by Alan Gottlieb
Printed and Bound in the United States by
Lake Book Manufacturing, Inc.

08 07 06 05 04
10 9 8 7 6 5 4 3 2 1

**Library of Congress
Cataloging-in-Publication Data**
Raum, Elizabeth.
  William Clark / by Elizabeth Raum.
     v. cm. -- (American lives)
Includes bibliographical references (p.) and index.
Contents: Redheaded Billy Clark -- Frontier life --
Soldier -- Trusted leader -- Called to explore --
Training the team -- Sacagawea -- Jefferson's map
maker -- Journey home -- Marriage and family --
Superintendent of Indians Affairs -- Governor --
Sand-haired chief. ISBN 1-4034-4194-4 -- ISBN 1-
4034-4202-9 (pbk.) 1. Clark, William, 1770-1838--
Juvenile literature. 2. Explorers--West (U.S.)--
Biography--Juvenile literature. 3. Lewis and Clark
Expedition (1804-1806)--Juvenile literature. 4. West
(U.S.)--Discovery and exploration--Juvenile
literature. 5. West (U.S.)--Biography--Juvenile
literature. [1. Clark, William, 1770-1838. 2.
Explorers. 3. Lewis and Clark Expedition (1804-
1806) 4. West (U.S.)--Discovery and exploration.] I.
Title. II. American lives (Heinemann Library
(Firm)) F592.7.C565R38 2003
  917.804'2'092--dc21
                    2003004973

Acknowledgments
The author and publishers are grateful to the
following for permission to reproduce copyright
material: Title page, pp. 4, 11 Independence
National Historical Park, Philadelphia; p. 5
Stepleton Collection/Corbis; pp. 6, 24 Filson
Historical Society, Louisville, Kentucky; pp. 7, 12
Michael Haynes Historic Art; p. 8 National
Museum of American History, Smithsonian
Institution, Washington, DC; pp. 9, 14 Hulton
Archive/Getty Images; p. 10 Chicago Historical
Society/Neg.# P&S-1914.1; pp. 13, 20 Library of
Congress; p. 15 Painting, Lewis and Clark: The
Departure from the Wood River Encampment, May
14, 1804, by Gary R. Lucy. Courtesy of the Gary R.
Lucy Gallery, Inc; p. 16 Joslyn Art Museum,
Omaha, Nebraska; pp. 17, 29 Smithsonian
American Art Museum, Washington, DC/Art
Resource, NY; pp. 18, 27 Bettmann/Corbis; pp. 19,
23, 25 Missouri Historical Society, St. Louis; p. 21
Wayne Mumford Photography; p. 22 Courtesy
American Antiquarian Society; p. 26 From the
Collections of the St. Louis Mercantile Library at
the University of Missouri-St. Louis; p. 28 National
Portrait Gallery, Smithsonian Institution/Art
Resource, NY

Cover photograph by Independence National
Historical Park, Philadelphia

The author thanks Sheldon Green, her friend and
colleague at Concordia College, Moorhead,
Minnesota, for sharing his expertise about the
journeys of Lewis and Clark.

The publisher would like to thank Michelle Rimsa
for her comments in the preparation of this book.

Every effort has been made to contact copyright
holders of any material reproduced in this book.
Any omissions will be rectified in subsequent
printings if notice is given to the publisher.

Some words are shown in bold, **like this.** You can
find out what they mean by looking in the glossary.

For more information on the image of William Clark
that appears on the cover of this book, turn to page 4.

Contents

Redheaded Billy Clark

There was a saying in the Clark family that every redheaded Clark would become famous. William Clark was the ninth child of John and Ann Rogers Clark. He was born on August 1, 1770, in Virginia. Little Billy's hair was bright red!

Two Clark brothers had red hair, and both became famous. George Rogers Clark, who was eighteen years older than Billy, became a famous soldier. Redheaded Billy Clark became a famous explorer, mapmaker, and peacekeeper.

William Clark accomplished many great things during his lifetime.

The **Revolutionary War** (1775–1783) began when Billy was only five years old. All five of Billy's brothers helped the United States win its freedom. His brother George became a hero by **conquering** the area which is now Illinois, Indiana, Ohio, Wisconsin, and Michigan. Young Billy listened to his brothers' stories of battle. He thought perhaps one day he would become a soldier, too.

George Rogers Clark became famous for his bravery during the Revolutionary War. He was an important **influence** in William's life.

Revolutionary War

*In 1776, the United States **declared** freedom from Britain. This resulted in a war that began in 1775 and lasted until 1783 when the United States won its freedom. This war was called the Revolutionary War.*

Frontier Life

Billy had very little formal schooling. At home he learned how to plant crops, trap, ride horses, and hunt.

Mulberry Hill, Will's home as a child, is now a **historical** site in Louisville, Kentucky.

When Billy, now called Will, was fourteen, the Clark family moved to Kentucky. It took them several months to reach their new home, Mulberry Hill. There were no schools on the Kentucky **frontier,** so Will's brother George taught him about plants and animals.

The Life of William Clark

1770	1784	1789	1804	1805
Born on August 1 in Virginia	*Moved to Kentucky*	*Joined militia*	*Left on expedition to the Pacific Ocean*	*Reached Pacific Ocean in November*

The **Revolutionary War** was over, but fighting continued on the Kentucky frontier. Britain, France, and Spain wanted North American land. They encouraged Native Americans to attack the settlers. Many farms and villages were burned, and the settlers were killed. The settlers decided to form a **militia** to fight back. Several of Will's brothers joined the militia. George Rogers Clark taught Will all about frontier fighting.

Will served in both the Kentucky militia and the U.S. Army before going on his **expedition** with Lewis.

1806	1807	1808	1813	1821	1838
Returned to St. Louis in September	*Became* **Superintendent of Indian Affairs**	*Married Julia Hancock*	*Became* **governor** *of Missouri Territory*	*Married Harriet Radford*	*Died on September 1*

Soldier

In 1789, when Will was nineteen, he joined the **militia.** He was good-looking, strong, and over six feet (eighteen meters) tall. He became a brave and fearless soldier who helped protect the settlers.

In 1791, Will joined the U.S. Army. He took over training and drilling soldiers and was made a **lieutenant.** He helped build **forts** and guide supply wagons to them.

This compass was probably the most important item Will used when guiding people. It told him what direction he was going.

"Cold," "verry Cold," and "excessively Cold" were the words Clark wrote in his journal to describe the weather during the winters. Hunting bears and making caps from their fur was one way to help the men stay warm.

Will took good care of the men under his command. During the winter of 1792, it was so cold that the soldier's cloth hats did not keep them warm. Will took the men bear hunting and helped them make warm bearskin caps. By spring, the militia reached Cincinnati, Ohio. Will bought new shoes, belt buckles, and a toothbrush. He even got a haircut. After several months in the woods, Will enjoyed his time in town.

Trusted Leader

People trusted Will Clark. He was able to gather helpful information for the army from French traders, Native American chiefs, and the leaders of Spanish **forts.** He kept careful notes about his travels and adventures.

Much of Clark's time in the army was spent ordering supplies and training soldiers. He became very good at making sure the men had enough food and supplies. He also learned about Native Americans. He understood their fear that white settlers were taking over so much of the land.

Members of the army tried to work with the Native Americans to settle arguments over the land.

In 1795, a young soldier named Meriwether Lewis joined Clark's rifle company. Clark and Lewis were together for about six months. Both men had grown up in Virginia, and both liked adventure. They became good friends.

Clark stayed in the army until 1796 when he returned to his family's Kentucky home. His brother George needed help. In 1799, Clark's father died and left him Mulberry Hill. Clark was not the oldest son, but he had the skills to manage Mulberry Hill. He also did not yet have a home of his own. Clark spent the next few years taking care of the farm.

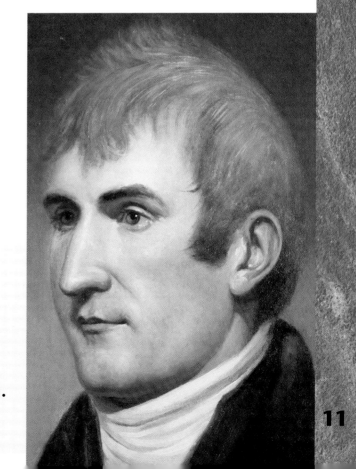

After leaving the army, Meriwether Lewis soon asked his friend Clark for help leading an **expedition.**

Called to Explore

In 1803, when Clark was 32 years old, he received a letter from Meriwether Lewis, his friend from the army. President Thomas Jefferson had asked Lewis to lead an **expedition** to the Pacific Ocean. Lewis invited Clark to join him. Lewis said they would both be captains, and they would lead the expedition together. Clark was excited. He told Lewis that he would join the expedition.

York was Clark's trusted slave who traveled everywhere with him.

Corps of Discovery

*Jefferson called the men on the expedition the **Corps** of Discovery. He hoped they would find a water route to the Pacific Ocean and that they would discover plants and animals that people in the eastern United States had never seen.*

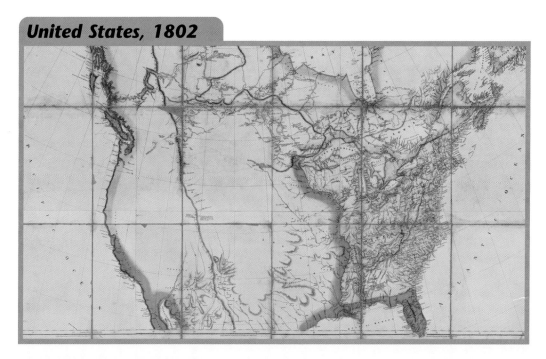

United States, 1802

Clark and Lewis went to places few had ever seen before. They relied on this map from 1802 to guide the way to the Pacific Ocean.

Clark's job was to find men willing to go on the expedition. He looked for men who were healthy, young, unmarried, and good at living in the wilderness. He needed men who were good hunters, so they could provide food.

Many men wanted to go, but Clark chose only the strongest and the bravest. He also decided to take York on the journey. York, an African-American slave, had been with Clark since they were both small boys. York was big and strong.

Training the Team

Clark enjoyed training the men. He led marches so the men would stay strong. He ordered the men to practice hunting by shooting at targets. Clark made sure that the men knew how important it was to obey orders. He sent hunters to find food while the rest of the men built a winter camp. It was too late in the year to begin the journey, so they spent the winter of 1804 near St. Louis, Missouri.

Whenever they stopped during their travels, Clark and his men built huts to live in.

The men of the expedition rowed their heavy boat up the Missouri River as they began their journey.

Clark's days were busy. He was in charge of building boats that would carry the men and supplies up the Missouri River. On May 14, 1804, Clark and his men headed out. They met up with Lewis on May 20. On May 21, the **expedition** began. Clark took charge of the boats and helped the men as they rowed up the muddy Missouri River. Travel was difficult on the river that Clark called the Big Muddy and that the Native Americans called Smokey Water.

Sacagawea

In October, the **expedition** reached the Mandan villages near present-day Bismarck, North Dakota. The captains decided to spend the winter there. The men were cold, and Clark helped the men build a small **fort** called Fort Mandan. Many Native Americans visited the fort. Some French-Canadian traders set up **tepees** nearby. One was Toussaint Charbonneau and his young Shoshoni wife, Sacagawea.

When the team reached the Mandan village, they had been traveling 164 days and gone 1,600 miles (2,575 km).

Charbonneau knew several Native American languages and agreed to serve as a guide for the expedition. Sacagawea helped by digging roots and gathering berries.

Clark liked Sacagawea and was kind to her. He called her Janey, an army term for "woman." Her baby, Jean Baptiste, was born in February 1805. Clark called him Pomp or Pompey because the baby liked to move around as if he was an

Sacagawea was an important part of the success of the expedition.

important leader giving orders. When the expedition headed west, the Charbonneau family joined them. Sacagawea, who also knew several Native American languages, helped by finding food and speaking with Native Americans they met on the trail.

Jefferson's Mapmaker

Clark kept a journal of the trip. President Jefferson wanted to see a written report, drawings, and maps from the journey. Even if he was tired or the weather was bad, Clark wrote notes to himself. Later, Clark used the notes to make longer journal entries. He measured the rivers and mountains, then drew the first maps of the western United States. The journals gave the world a written account of the people, animals, and plants in the West.

Sacagawea helped by leading the **expedition** in the right direction to reach the Pacific Ocean.

President Jefferson hoped that the Missouri River led to the Pacific Ocean. Lewis and Clark discovered that it did not. Without a river, Clark and his men needed horses to cross the mountains. Clark bought 29 horses from Cameahwait, Sacagawea's Shoshoni brother, so that they could cross the Rocky Mountains. The journey was difficult.

Clark's journals contained important information about what was discovered during the expedition.

They ran out of food and became ill. When they reached the Columbia River, Clark helped the men build canoes to carry them to the Pacific Ocean.

Because there were no maps, Lewis and Clark had trouble finding the ocean. They split up. Lewis and a small group found the Pacific on November 14, 1805. On November 18, Clark and his group followed their trail and reached the Pacific Ocean as well.

Journey Home

The men spent the winter camped by the Columbia River. Many Native Americans visited them. Clark wrote in his journal that it was rainy and wet. The team ran out of food. Clark took several men and Sacagawea to the ocean to see a whale that had washed ashore. Everyone was amazed by the size of the animal. Although the group was very eager to return home, they had to wait until the mountain snow melted.

Lewis and Clark Trail, 1814

This map shows the path Clark and his men took across the **frontier.** The journey took the men two years, four months, and nine days. They traveled 6,000 miles (9,656 km).

Pompey's Pillar still stands in Montana today. Clark's signature, the day, and date remain visible on the pillar's rock face.

After the difficult trip across the Rocky Mountains, Lewis and Clark separated. Clark explored the Yellowstone River in Montana. On July 25, 1806, he discovered a 100-foot-tall (30 m) sandstone **butte.** He named it Pompey's Pillar in honor of little Pomp. When they reached the Mandan villages, Clark said good-bye to the Charbonneaus. He offered to take Pomp home with him and send him to school. Sacagawea promised to bring Pomp to live with Clark when he was older.

Marriage and Family

When the team arrived in St. Louis on September 23, 1806, Clark was greeted as a hero. Crowds gathered and people cheered. Clark returned to Kentucky to visit his family. He did not stay long because he was eager to see a woman named Julia Hancock. They had been **courting** before the trip. Clark asked her to marry him. Julia said yes, but before the wedding, President Jefferson asked Clark to travel to Kentucky to oversee a **fossil** dig.

By the last Mails.

MARYLAND. BALTIMORE, OCT. 29, 1806

A LETTER from St. Louis (Upper Louisiana) dated Sept. 23, 1806, announces the arrival of Captains LEWIS and CLARK, from their expedition into the interior.—They went to the *Pacific Ocean*, have brought some of the natives and curiosities of the countries through which they passed, and only lost one man. They left the *Pacific Ocean* 23d March, 1806, where they arrived in November 1805;—and where some American vessels had been just before.—They state the Indians to be as numerous on the *Columbia* river, which empties into the *Pacific*, as the whites in any part of the U. S. They brought a family of the Mandan indians with them. The winter was very mild on the *Pacific*.—They have kept an ample journal of their tour; which will be published, and must afford much intelligence.

People had given up hope on the **expedition,** so they were very excited when the group returned.

Clark's Firsts

William Clark was the first American explorer to:

- *measure rivers and mountains in the West*
- *map the route from the Missouri River to the Pacific Ocean*
- *explore the Yellowstone River*

Pomp

When Sacagawea's son Pomp was four or five years old, his parents brought him to St. Louis. Toussaint Charbonneau and Sacagawea left him with Clark while they went on a fur-trading expedition. In 1812, after Sacagawea died, Clark adopted Pomp and his baby sister, Lisette. He gave Pomp a place to live, paid for his education, and acted like a father toward him.

On January 5, 1808, Clark married Julia Hancock. They moved to St. Louis. Meriwether Lewis often visited them. When William and Julia's first son was born a year later, they named the baby Meriwether Lewis Clark in honor of Clark's good friend and fellow explorer.

Julia Hancock was 16 when she married Clark. Clark was 37 years old.

Superintendent of Indian Affairs

President Jefferson rewarded the **expedition** captains with land and money. He put Clark in charge of the Louisiana **militia** and named him **Superintendent of Indian Affairs.** Clark took control of the army in the Louisiana **Territory.** He built a **fort** called Fort Osage. Every boat passing on the river could be seen from Fort Osage. He met with Native American leaders and listened to their ideas.

The Native Americans who met Clark respected him for his honesty.

After spending so much time in the wilderness, Clark came home to a large, comfortable house in St. Louis.

In 1812, war broke out between the British and the Americans. Clark convinced several Native American chiefs to join the fight against the British. Clark tried to keep peace with the Native Americans. Both the eastern **politicians** and the Native American chiefs felt they could trust Clark. He liked Native Americans, and they accepted him as their friend. They called him the Redhaired Chief. The war ended in 1814 with no clear winner.

Governor

In 1813, Clark was appointed **governor** of the Missouri **Territory.** As governor, he continued to work with Native Americans. In 1815, he helped to make peace with nineteen tribes at Portage des Sioux in Missouri. The next year, he met with ten more tribes who also agreed to the terms of peace. Much of his work involved keeping peace between Native American groups and protecting settlers.

Clark was renamed as governor three times before Missouri became a state in 1821.

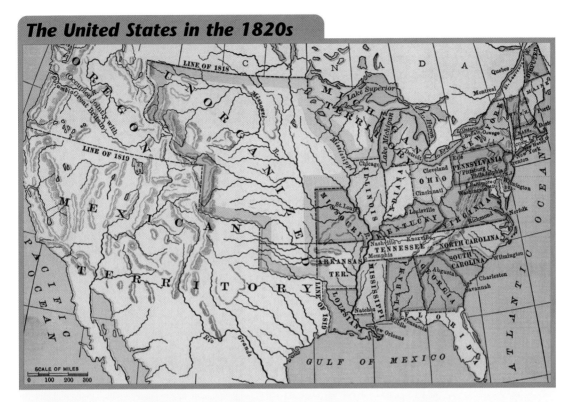

In 1826, the land was still divided between Mexico and the United States.

Clark was sad to see Native Americans and settlers fighting over land. Sometimes Clark had to remove white settlers who stole Native American land. Sometimes Native Americans sold land to white settlers and then tried to take it back. Clark had to stop them from taking it back. He always tried to be kind and gentle with both groups. He never raised his voice in anger.

Sand-Haired Chief

Julia and William Clark had four sons and one daughter. Even though Clark did everything possible to help Julia, she became ill and died in 1820. Clark was very lonely without Julia. In 1821, he married her cousin, Harriet Radford. They had two children together.

As Clark grew older, his red hair turned gray. Native American chiefs who visited him in St. Louis began to call him the Sand-Haired Chief. They brought him presents of clothing, weapons, and handmade crafts. He displayed them in a museum near his home.

Until his death in 1838, Clark fought for fair treatment of Native Americans.

This is one of George Catlin's paintings from the 1830s. Other paintings of his are on pages 17 and 28.

Many famous people visited Clark in St. Louis, including Daniel Boone, the **frontiersman** who first explored and settled Kentucky, and George Catlin, who painted beautiful pictures of frontier life.

At age 68, William Clark moved in with his son Meriwether. He died on September 1, 1838, after a short illness. The people of St. Louis said good-bye. Hundreds came to his funeral, and guns were fired into the air to honor a man who was a true American hero.

Glossary

butte steep hill standing alone

conquering winning by fighting

corps group of people working together

courting formal dating of another, with the intent to marry

declare say clearly or announce

expedition journey taken for a special purpose

fort strong building used for defense against enemy attack

fossil remains of an ancient plant or animal that have turned to stone

frontier unsettled area of a country. A person who explores the frontier is called a *frontiersman*.

governor person who is in charge of a state or territory

historical important in history

influence be important to and have an effect on another

lieutenant military officer

militia group of soldiers called to fight in an emergency

politician someone who works for the government and represents people

Revolutionary War war from 1775 to 1783 in which the American colonists won freedom from Great Britain

Superintendent of Indian Affairs person appointed to work with Native Americans

tepee tent shaped like an upside-down ice cream cone

territory part of the United States that is not yet a state

More Books to Read

Isaacs, Sally Senzell. *America in the Time of Lewis and Clark*. Chicago: Heinemann Library, 1999.

Kline, Trish. *Lewis and Clark*. Vero Beach, Fl.: Rourke, 2002.

Ransom, Candice. *Lewis and Clark*. Minneapolis: Lerner Publications, 2003.

Witteman, Barbara. *Sacagawea*. Mankato, Minn.: Bridgestone Books, 2002.

Places to Visit

Fort Clatsop National Memorial (reconstructed fort)
Astoria, Oregon
Visitor Information: (503) 861-2471

Jefferson National Expansion Memorial
11 North 4th Street
St. Louis, Missouri 63102
Visitor Information: (314) 655-1700

The North Dakota Lewis & Clark Interpretive Center
P.O. Box 607
Washburn, ND 58577-0607
Visitor Information: (701) 462-8535

Pompey's Pillar
Billings, Montana
Visitor Information: (406) 875-2233

Index